Aunt Phil's Trunk

Teacher Guide

for

The Call of the Wild
and
Other Northland Stories

BY
JACK LONDON

Jack London's Journey to Fame and Fortune
By Laurel Downing Bill

Front Cover Art by Kim Sherry

Teacher Guide

for

The Call of the Wild

and

Other Northland Stories

STORIES BY
JACK LONDON

CURRICULUM BY
LAUREL DOWNING BILL

Special thanks to Nicole Cruz for her assitance in makng this teacher guide and its accompanying student workbook for
The Call of the Wild and Other Northland Stories

Aunt Phil's Trunk LLC, Anchorage, Alaska
www.auntphilstrunk.com
Copyright © 2017 by Laurel Downing Bill
Reprinted 2023

All rights reserved. No part of this book may be used or reproduced in any manner whatsoever without written permission from the author, except in the case of brief quotations embodied in critical articles and reviews

ISBN: 978-1-940479-17-0

Instructions for using *The Call of the Wild and Other Northland Stories* Curriculum

The Call of the Wild and Other Northland Stories curriculum is designed to be used as part of a ninth- or tenth-grade language arts curriculum. Students will begin by reading and analyzing one of Jack London's classic novels, *The Call of the Wild*. Reading one chapter at a time, students will learn new vocabulary words and answer comprehension and discussion questions for each chapter. They will explore the meaning of key quotes from the chapter and analyze the main theme of the reading. Each lesson concludes with a writing exercise to encourage deeper interaction with the text, as well as practice creative writing skills.

In the second section of the curriculum, students will read several of Jack London's short stories. Each lesson includes vocabulary words, discussion questions, key quotes from the story and an opportunity to write a short summary of the story. The writing exercises in this unit encourage creative writing and some imitation of techniques used by London.

The curriculum concludes with a lesson on the life of Jack London. Students will begin by reading several short chapters to learn about his life. Next, students will answer comprehension and discussion questions about the reading. The lesson concludes with a final essay on one of three options.

I hope that you and your students enjoy this journey into the life and stories of one of America's most beloved authors, Jack London.

NOTE: Racial slurs in *A Thousand Deaths* by Jack London

Teachers/parents: Please note that sometimes Jack London uses racial slurs in his writing. Especially in the final short story that students will read in this curriculum titled, *A Thousand Deaths*. The presence of words of this type in this curriculum in no way condones the use of them. We wanted this story included in this collection because it is the story that basically launched London's career as a writer in 1899.

While compiling this collection of stories, we considered changing some words to reflect how attitudes have changed since London wrote his works. But we felt it more important to keep his writings in tact as he first wrote them.

Consider using this opportunity to open up a dialogue about why London may have used such terms in 1899, and why it is not typical to see these terms in modern literature. Most importantly, you can discuss why these words are hurtful and unacceptable for anyone to use in any context. After all …

"Those who cannot remember the past are condemned to repeat it."
– George Santayana

GRADING: Instructions for grading students' work and Rubric grids begin on page 84.

Jack London (b. Jan. 12, 1876 – d. Nov. 22, 1916) was a prolific fiction writer. Many people got their first glimpse of life in the northland by reading his stories of the Klondike.

TABLE OF CONTENTS

The Call of the Wild
Lesson 1 – Into the Primitive	6
Lesson 2 – The Law of Club and Fang	10
Lesson 3 – The Dominant Primordial	14
Lesson 4 – Who Has Won to Mastership	18
Lesson 5 – The Toil of Trace and Trail	22
Lesson 6 – For the Love of a Man	26
Lesson 7 – The Sounding of the Call	30
Wild Vocabulary Crossword Puzzle	34

Other Northland Stories
To the Man on the Trail	36
The White Silence	40
The Son of the Wolf	44
The Men of Forty Mile	48
In a Far Country	52
The Priestly Prerogative	56
The Wife of the King	60
The Wisdom of the Trail	64
An Odyssey of the North	68
To Build a Fire	72

Jack London's Journey
Toward Fame and Fortune/In His Own Words	76
Final Essay	79
Northland Vocabulary Crossword Puzzle	82

Grading
Rubric Grid Instructions	84
Rubric Grids	85
Grading Sheets	87

THE CALL OF THE WILD

LESSON 1: INTO THE PRIMITIVE

BEFORE YOU READ

Quote from the Reading

Look for this quote in your reading and pay special attention to its context:

"London's message that civilization is a thin veneer that can, under certain circumstances, disappear and return one to a wild state is as relevant today as it was when he wrote this story more than 100 years ago." – From the introduction

VOCABULARY

Look for these words in your reading:

Primitive – belonging to or characteristic of an early stage of development
Demesne – domain; land actually possessed by the lord of an estate and not held by tenants
Insular – protected; inexperienced
Calamity – an event that causes great harm; deep distress or misery
Dormant – not active but capable of becoming active

READING

Read: Introduction, Cast of Characters and Chapter 1 in your textbook (Pages 5-17)

NOW THAT YOU'VE READ THE ASSIGNED CHAPTER

After reading Chapter 1, what do you think the author meant by the quote above? *Answers will vary.*

_____
_____
_____
_____
_____
_____
_____
_____

COMPREHENSION

1) Where does the beginning of the story take place? Why did Jack London choose this setting to open his book?
The Call of the Wild begins on a California estate in the Santa Clara Valley. Jack London had actually visited the Bond farm, as the Bonds were friends he had made while seeking his fortune in the Klondike during 1897-1898. (Pages 5 and 8)

2) Who is the main character of the book? What do we learn about this character in Chapter 1?
A Saint Bernard-Scotch Shepard mix named Buck is the main character of the story. In Chapter 1, we learn that Buck has a good life on the ranch where he is treated well and rules the land. He is trusting of men until he is kidnapped by Manuel. We learn that he has strong instincts to survive and can be violent when provoked. (Answers will vary)

3) Who was Manuel? Why did he steal Buck?
Manuel is an underpaid gardener's helper who could not support his wife, children or his gambling habit. Manuel seizes the opportunity to make some quick cash by kidnapping Buck and selling him as a sled dog during the infamous rush to the Klondike gold fields during 1897-1898. (Page 6)

4) How does the man with the red sweater treat Buck? Why?
The man with the red sweater beat Buck with a club to show him that man is the boss and in order to teach him the primitive law. (Page 14)

DISCUSSION

What is the significance of the title of Chapter 1?
Answers will vary.

WRITING EXERCISE

As you read in the introduction, Jack London based *The Call of the Wild* on places and people that he met in his life. The main character, Buck, closely resembled a dog that the Bond family loaned to the author while he was in the Klondike. Great fiction often comes from our life experiences. Write a one-page short story that is inspired by a place or an event that is special to you. Try to convey your feelings about the place or the event in your writing.

THE CALL OF THE WILD

LESSON 2: THE LAW OF CLUB AND FANG

BEFORE YOU READ

Quote from the Reading

Look for this quote in your reading and pay special attention to its context:

"He had been suddenly jerked from the heart of civilization and flung into the heart of things primordial."

VOCABULARY

Look for these words in your reading:

Diabolically – with evil intent
Primordial – first created or developed
Dignity – quality or state of being worthy or esteemed
Disconsolate – very sad
Antagonist – one who contends with or opposes another

READING

Read: Chapter 2 (Pages 18-26)

NOW THAT YOU'VE READ THE ASSIGNED CHAPTER

Who was the quote above about? Rewrite it in your own words.
Answers will vary, but the quote was about Buck being taken from "civilization" at the ranch and taken into the "wild" of the Yukon. (Page 18)

COMPREHENSION

1) What tragedy occurred on Buck's first day in the Yukon? What did he learn from it?
Curly was attacked and killed by the other dogs. Buck learned that other dogs were savages and that he needed to fight to stay alive. He learned that life in the Yukon was very different from his life back on the ranch where life was peaceful. (Page 18)

2) What dogs did Buck meet in Chapter 2? Describe them.
Buck met Billee, Joe and Sol-leks. Billee and Joe were brothers. Billee's one fault was his excessive good nature, while Joe was the very opposite, sour and introspective, with a perpetual snarl and a malignant eye. Sol-leks (means the angry one) was an old husky, long and lean and gaunt, with a battle-scarred face and a single eye that flashed a warning of prowess that commanded respect. (Pages 19-20)

3) What was the law of club and fang? How was this different from the laws that Buck previously lived by on Judge Miller's ranch?
The law of the club and fang was that you had to fight to survive. If you did not fight, steal, and take care of yourself, you will die. You had to obey the correction of the club and the fang to survive. In Buck's life on the ranch, he was able to do as he pleased and could trust the humans to provide and care for him.

4) Describe how Buck learns to become a sled dog.
Buck learned how to become a sled dog when Francois put a harness on him and used a whip to bring correction. Dave and Spitz corrected Buck by nipping at his heels and growling at him. (Page 19)

DISCUSSION

Jack London tells the story from the point of view of the main character, Buck. How do you think this story would be different if it was told from the point of view of a human character?
(Answers will vary)

WRITING EXERCISE

The term "point of view" originates from the Latin phrase, punctum visus, which means "position from which a thing is viewed." By using the point of view of an animal, Jack London gives a unique interpretation of the events that occur in this fictional tale. Choose one of your favorite stories and rewrite a scene from it using the point of view of an animal.

THE CALL OF THE WILD
LESSON 3: THE DOMINANT PRIMORDIAL BEAST

BEFORE YOU READ
Quote from the Reading
Look for this quote in your reading and pay special attention to its context:

"The dark circle became a dot on the moon-flooded snow as Spitz disappeared from view. Buck stood and looked on, the successful champion, the dominant primordial beast who had made his kill and found it good."

VOCABULARY
Look for these words in your reading:

Marauders – one who roams about in search of things to steal
Covert – not openly made or done
Insidious – sinister; dangerous
Supremacy – supreme power or authority
Inexorable – unstoppable or relentless

READING
Read: Chapter 3 (Pages 27-39)

NOW THAT YOU'VE READ THE ASSIGNED CHAPTER
What do you think the author meant when he called Buck a "dominant primordial beast" in the quote above?
(Answers will vary, but Buck had just asserted his dominance over Spitz to take leadership of the team. (Page 39)

COMPREHENSION

1) How do Buck and Spitz become rivals?
Spitz bullied Buck by constantly picking fights with him. After Spitz took Buck's nest, Buck decided that he had enough of Spitz' bullying and attacked him. The fight was broken up by a pack of wild dogs that entered the camp in search of food. (Pages 27-29)

2) Describe the wild dogs that were searching for food at the camp. How were they different than any dog that Buck had ever seen?
It seemed as though their bones would burst through their skins. They were mere skeletons, draped loosely in draggled hides, with blazing eyes and slavered fangs. But the hunger-madness made them terrifying, irresistible. (Pages 28-29)

3) In what ways do Francois and Perrault show compassion for the dogs in this chapter?
Francois and Perrault often put the dog's welfare ahead of their own. Francois killed Dolly to save Buck. He saved Buck again when Spitz attacked him after he collapsed from exhaustion.

4) Describe the fight at the end of the chapter between Buck and Spitz.
As the pack is hunting a rabbit, Spitz cuts off Buck and gets to the rabbit first. Buck attacks Spitz and realizes that they are going to fight to the death. Spitz is the more experienced fighter and seems to be winning the fight until Buck tricks Spitz, breaks his legs, and finishes him off in front of a circle of dogs. (Pages 37-38)

DISCUSSION

Do you think that Buck's time on the Yukon prepared him for this fight with Spitz? Do you think that Buck would have won the fight if it had happened before he was kidnapped and taken to the Yukon? *(Answers will vary)*

WRITING EXERCISE

Have you ever experienced a bully like Spitz? Write about a time that you or someone you know was bullied. Describe the bully and at least one interaction with the bully. How did the person being bullied respond? Conclude with your thoughts on the best way to handle being bullied.

THE CALL OF THE WILD

LESSON 4: WHO HAS WON TO MASTERSHIP

BEFORE YOU READ

Quote from the Reading

Look for this quote in your reading and pay special attention to its context:

"But it was in giving the law and making his mates live up to it that Buck excelled."

VOCABULARY

Look for these words in your reading:

Manifested – clear to the senses
Obdurate – stubborn
Lugubriously – sadly
Perplexed – confused

READING

Read: Chapter 4 (Pages 40-47)

NOW THAT YOU'VE READ THE ASSIGNED CHAPTER

The quote above describes the kind of leader that Buck became in Chapter 4. How would you describe Buck as a leader?

(Answers will vary)

COMPREHENSION

1) How did Francois and Perrault react when they discovered that Buck killed Spitz? Which dog did they choose to make lead dog? What did Buck do about this?
Francois and Perrault did not seem upset. They thought that they would make better time without Spitz. They chose Sol-leks to be lead dog, but Buck made it clear that he wanted to be lead dog. They tried to force Buck into place, but eventually gave in when they realized they were behind schedule. (Pages 41-42)

2) What happened when the team got to Skagway?
Francois called Buck to him, threw his arms around him, wept over him. And that was the last of Francois and Perrault. A Scotch half-breed took charge of Buck and his mates, and in company with a dozen other dog teams he started back over the weary trail to Dawson. (Page 43)

3) Describe the man that Buck "sees" by the fire. Who or what do you think this man symbolizes?
This other man was shorter of leg and longer of arm, with muscles that were stringy and knotty rather than rounded and swelling. The hair of this man was long and matted, and his head slanted back under it from the eyes. He was all but naked, a ragged and fire-scorched skin hanging partway down his back, but on his body there was much hair. The man symbolizes Buck's introduction to his primitive side. (Pages 44-45)

4) Why did the new owner shoot Dave at the end of the chapter?
Dave was suffering and dying. He was no longer able to continue with the other dogs. (Page 47)

DISCUSSION

If you could choose one word to describe Dave's death, what would it be? Why?
(Answers will vary)

WRITING EXERCISE

Authors often use dreams to communicate or highlight an important theme in the story, just as Jack London used Buck's dream of a hairy, rugged man to symbolize a key theme in his story. Write a short fictional story that centers around a dream.

THE CALL OF THE WILD

LESSON 5: THE TOIL OF TRACE AND TRAIL

BEFORE YOU READ

Quote from the Reading

Look for this quote in your reading and pay special attention to its context:

"The wonderful patience of the trail that comes to men who toil hard and suffer sore, and remain sweet of speech and kindly, did not come to these two men and the woman."

VOCABULARY

Look for these words in your reading:

Salient – important
Jaded – dull; apathetic
Slovenly – untidy
Voracious – very powerful
Inarticulate – difficulty expressing with words

READING

Read: Chapter 5 (Pages 48-61)

NOW THAT YOU'VE READ THE ASSIGNED CHAPTER

Who is the quote above about? What do you think the author meant by this?
Answers will vary, but this quote was about Hal, Charles and Mercedes. They were lazy, disorganized and reckless. They were constantly bickering and not patient. (Page 55)

COMPREHENSION

1) Describe Hal and Charles.
Charles was a middle-aged, lightish-colored man, with weak and watery eyes and a mustache that twisted fiercely and vigorously up. Hal was a youngster of nineteen or twenty, with a big Colt's revolver and a hunting knife strapped about him on a belt that fairly bristled with cartridges. The two men looked out of place. (Pages 48-49)

2) What did Buck think about his new owners?
Buck felt vaguely that there was no depending upon these two men and the woman. They did not know how to do anything, and as the days went by it became apparent that they could not learn. They were slack in all things, without order or discipline. Buck and his comrades looked upon them with disgust. (Page 53)

3) What were some of the reasons that Hal, Charles and Mercedes were behind schedule?
The dogs were tired from the trip to Skagway and needed rest, but Hal and Charles decided to force them to travel. The dogs were hungry because they decided to overfeed them in order to strengthen them, which didn't work, and eventually they ran out of food.

4) Why did Buck refuse to lead the team?
He had made up his mind not to get up. He had a vague feeling of impending doom. This had been strong upon him when he pulled in to the bank, and it had not departed from him. With the thin and rotten ice he had felt under his feet all day, it seemed that he sensed disaster close at hand, out there ahead on the ice where his master was trying to drive him. (Page 59)

DISCUSSION

Reread the opening four lines of Chapter 1. These lines are from a poem by John Meyers O'Hara called "Atavism" that Jack London thought reflected the theme of The Call of the Wild. Do you agree with him? Explain why or why not?
(Answers will vary)

_____
_____
_____
_____
_____
_____
_____
_____

WRITING EXERCISE

How would you summarize the theme of *The Call of the Wild* for someone who hasn't read the book yet? Write a poem that reflects your thoughts.

THE CALL OF THE WILD

LESSON 6: FOR THE LOVE OF A MAN

BEFORE YOU READ

Quote from the Reading

Look for this quote in your reading and pay special attention to its context:

"He was older than the days he had seen and the breaths he had drawn."

VOCABULARY

Look for these words in your reading:

Eloquent – forceful or fluent expression
Reverently – very respectful
Transient – not lasting or staying too long
Tenderfoot – a beginner

READING

Read: Chapter 6 (Pages 62-74)

NOW THAT YOU'VE READ THE ASSIGNED CHAPTER

What do you think the author meant by the quote above?
(Answers will vary)

COMPREHENSION

1) Was Buck's relationship with John Thornton different than his relationship with his other owners? Explain your answer.
Yes. Buck felt a "genuine passionate love" for John Thornton that he never felt before. (Pages 62-63)

2) How did Buck show his affection for John Thornton?
He would often seize Thornton's hand in his mouth and close so fiercely that the flesh bore the impress of his teeth for some time afterward. And as Buck understood the oaths to be love words, so the man understood this feigned bite for a caress. For the most part, however, Buck's love was expressed in adoration. He would lie by the hour, eager, alert, at Thornton's feet, looking up into his face, dwelling upon it, studying it. (Page 63)

3) Describe one of the two times that Buck saved John Thornton's life.
a) Buck protected him when "Black" Burton attacked John at a Circle City bar. Buck bit the man in the throat, almost killing him.
b) Buck also saved John's life when he fell off his boat into a bad stretch of rapids. Pete and Hans tied a rope around Buck and John held onto Buck until they pulled him ashore. (Pages 69-71)

4) What bet did John Thornton make? Did he win the bet?
John bet $1,000 that Buck could break from the ice and pull a 1,000-pound sled. Buck sensed that he could do something good for John Thornton, so he completed the task. John won the bet. (Pages 70-73)

DISCUSSION

What similarities do you see between Buck and John Thornton?
(Answers will vary)

WRITING EXERCISE

Write a poem, song or letter from Buck to John Thornton explaining his call to the wild. Try to convey Buck's feelings of wanting to stay loyal to John, yet still needing to abide by the law of club and fang.

THE CALL OF THE WILD

LESSON 7: THE SOUNDING OF THE CALL

BEFORE YOU READ

Quote from the Reading

Look for this quote in your reading and pay special attention to its context:

"He knew he was at last answering the call, running by the side of his wood brother toward the place from where the call surely came."

VOCABULARY

Look for these words in your reading:

Ramshackle – run-down
Formidable – causing fear or dread
Sequential – in order
Muses – to ponder or reflect
Discomfited – to put into a state of perplexity or embarrassment

READING

Read: Chapter 7 (Pages 75-89)

NOW THAT YOU'VE READ THE ASSIGNED CHAPTER

What do you think the author meant by the quote above?
(Answers will vary)

COMPREHENSION

1) What adventure did Buck, John and his partners go on after John won the bet? Did Buck enjoy this adventure?
John, Hans and Pete went in search of a lost mine. To Buck it was boundless delight, this hunting, fishing and indefinite wandering through strange places. (Page 75)

2) What happened when Buck met a timber wolf in the woods?
Buck chased the timber wolf until he realized that Buck meant him no harm. He wanted to be friends. Buck ran with the wolf until he felt the call to go back to John Thornton. (Pages 78-80)

3) How did his love of John Thornton cause Buck to "lose his head"?
After killing a moose, Buck returned to the camp to find John Thornton, Hans, Pete and the dogs had all been killed by a band of Yeehats. He went into a rage, killing several men and then retreated to the forest. (Pages 85-87)

4) Jack London uses many events throughout the book to foreshadow the ending. Were you surprised by the ending? Were there any events that might have given you a clue to the ending?
(Answers will vary)

DISCUSSION

After completing the novel, which characters would you call wild? Which characters would you call civilized? Explain why.
(Answers will vary)

WRITING EXERCISE

The Call of the Wild is considered a great piece of literature. What do you consider to be three characteristics of a great novel? Write a persuasive letter to a friend who is not interested in reading *The Call of the Wild*. Explain why *The Call of the Wild* is a great novel using those three characteristics and supporting details from the novel.

Wild Vocabulary
Crossword Puzzle

Read the Across and Down clues and fill in the blank boxes that match the number on the clues

ACROSS

5 Forceful or fluent expression
6 First created or developed
9 Very powerful
13 With evil intent
16 Quality or state of being worthy or esteemed
19 One who contends with or opposes another
22 Not active but capable of becoming active
25 In order
26 Confused
27 Unstoppable or relentless
28 Stubborn
30 To ponder or reflect
31 An event that causes great harm; deep distress or misery
32 Belonging to or characteristic of an early stage of development
33 Untidy

DOWN

1 Not openly made or done
2 Supreme power or authority
3 Protected; inexperienced
4 Causing fear or dread
7 Difficulty expressing with words
8 To put into a state of perplexity or embarrassment
10 Very sad
11 Sinister; dangerous
12 Run-down
14 Sadly
15 Clear to the senses
17 Not lasting or staying too long
18 Domain; land actually possessed by the lord of an estate and not held by tenants
20 A beginner
21 One who roams about in search of things to steal
23 Important
24 Very respectful
29 Dull; apathetic

Wild Vocabulary
Crossword Puzzle Key

Read the Across and Down clues and fill in the blank boxes that match the number on the clues

35

NORTHLAND STORIES

LESSON 8: TO THE MAN ON THE TRAIL

BEFORE YOU READ

Quote from the Reading

Look for this quote in your reading and pay special attention to its context:

"It was evident that they were angry – first, at the way they had been deceived; and second, at the outraged ethics of the Northland, where honesty, above all, was man's prime jewel."

VOCABULARY

Look for these words in your reading:

Benignantly – showing kindly feelings or intentions
Pertinacity – stubbornly or annoyingly persistent
Monotonous – boring from being always the same

READING

Read: *To the Man on the Trail* (Pages 90-99)

NOW THAT YOU'VE READ THE ASSIGNED STORY

Reread the quote above. To whom is the author referring? Why are they angry?
<u>Answers will vary, but the author is referring to the men in the bar who were angry that they didn't know that Jack Westondale had stolen money and was on the run from the police.</u> *(Page 98)*

STORY SUMMARY

Summarize *To the Man on the Trail* below. How would you describe the theme of this story?

Answers will vary. Students may include some of the points below:
Malemute Kid and a group of miners spent time talking about life in the Northland. Jack Westondale walked into the Kid's place and traded stories with Malemute Kid about their travels and family back in the states. After the men saw him off, a young policeman came in looking for Jack because he had stolen $40,000. Malemute Kid did not want to help the officer, because he knew that Jack took money that was stolen from him by Joe Castrell.

DISCUSSION

After reading this short story and the *Call of the Wild*, how would you describe life for an adventurer in the Northland? What words come to mind? *(Answers will vary)*

WRITING EXERCISE

Write your own song or poem about life as an adventurer in the Northland. Use some of the words that you brainstormed in the discussion question. You will receive a bonus point for every vocabulary word you include.

NORTHLAND STORIES

LESSON 9: THE WHITE SILENCE

BEFORE YOU READ

Quote from the Reading

Look for this quote in your reading and pay special attention to its context:

"Don't send her back to her people, Kid. It's beastly hard for a woman to go back."

VOCABULARY

Look for these words in your reading:

Ruefully – pity or sympathy
Propinquity – nearness in place or time
Primeval – relating to a primitive or early age

READING

Read: *The White Silence* (Pages 100-108)

NOW THAT YOU'VE READ THE ASSIGNED STORY

Reread the quote above. Who said this quote? What did he mean by this statement?
<u>Anwers will vary. Mason said this quote to Kid. He was asking him not to send his wife, Ruth, back to her tribe because she wouldn't adjust well to going back to the lifestyle of her people after living the life of a white man's wife.</u> *(Page 105)*

STORY SUMMARY

Summarize *White Silence* below. How would you describe the theme of this story?
Answers will vary. Students may include some of the points below:
White Silence is about three adventurers – Malemute Kid, Mason and his pregnant wife, Ruth. As they are traveling by dog sled across the Yukon, one of their dogs, Carmen, becomes very weak. Mason forces the dog to continue by whipping it badly. As he stops his sled, a pine tree comes down on him and breaks his back, leg and arm. He tells Malemute Kid to continue without him to save his wife and child.

DISCUSSION

Why do you think the author titled this story, "White Silence"? *(Answers will vary)*

WRITING EXERCISE

Write a short essay that answers these questions:
1) Are you beginning to see common themes among Jack London's writings? If so, what are they?
2) Can you think of another story written by a different author that shares a similar theme? Include specific examples from the stories to support your answer.

NORTHLAND STORIES

LESSON 10: THE SON OF THE WOLF

BEFORE YOU READ

Quote from the Reading

Look for this quote in your reading and pay special attention to its context:

"If, in the days to come, thou shouldst journey to the Country of the Yukon, know thou that there shall always be a place and much food by the fire of the Wolf. The night is now passing into the day. I go, but I may come again. And for the last time, remember the Law of the Wolf!"

VOCABULARY

Look for these words in your reading:

Malady – a disease or disorder of the body or mind
Anomaly – something different, abnormal or strange
Anachronism – a person or a thing out of place in time

READING

Read: *The Son of the Wolf* (Pages 110-124)

NOW THAT YOU'VE READ THE ASSIGNED STORY

Reread the quote above. What was the "law of the wolf"?
According to Mackenzie, the law of the wolf is: "Whoso taketh the life of one Wolf, the forfeit shall ten of his people pay. In many lands has the price been paid; in many lands shall it yet be paid." (Pages 121,124)

STORY SUMMARY

Summarize *The Son of the Wolf* below. How would you describe the theme of this story?
Answers will vary. Students may include some of the points below:
Mackenzie was a lonely adventurer who wanted to make the daughter of the Chief of the Tanana people his wife. He did all he could to impress the tribe and Zarinska. Zarinska agreed to be his wife, but her father did not agree to the marriage. Mackenzie and the Chief threatened one another, and the Chief eventually gave in to Mackenzie's demand but gave him a warning. Before Mackenzie could leave, a young man named Bear challenged Mackinze and they fought for Zarinska. Mackenzie told the tribe of the "law of the wolf" as he left with Zarinska.

DISCUSSION

Why do you think the Tanana people called Mackenzie "Son of Wolf"?
(Answers will vary)

WRITING EXERCISE

Compare and contrast the cultures of Mackenzie and Zarinska. Can you find any similarities between the two? How are they different? How do the differences impact both Mackenzie and Zarinksa? Write a short essay answering each of these questions.

NORTHLAND STORIES

LESSON 11: THE MEN OF FORTY MILE

BEFORE YOU READ

Quote from the Reading

Look for this quote in your reading and pay special attention to its context:

"There was no law in the land. The mounted police was also a thing of the future. Each man measured an offense, and meted out the punishment inasmuch as it affected himself."

VOCABULARY

Look for these words in your reading:

Caste – a division of society based upon differences of wealth, rank, or occupation
Remonstrances – an act or instance of protest
Paradoxal – contradictory or opposed to common sense

READING

Read: *The Men of Forty Mile* (Pages 125-133)

NOW THAT YOU'VE READ THE ASSIGNED STORY

Reread the quote above. How do you think the story would be different if there were mounted police? *(Answers will vary)*

_____
_____
_____
_____
_____
_____
_____
_____
_____
_____
_____
_____
_____

STORY SUMMARY

Summarize *The Men of Forty Mile* below. *(Answers will vary)*

DISCUSSION

Imagine that you are a friend of Bettles and Lon in the story. What would you do to try to stop them from fighting? *(Answers will vary)*

WRITING EXERCISE

Jack London often employs the use of different dialects in his stories to make his characters more authentic. Write your own short story that takes place anywhere in the world. Include at least one scene where the characters speak in a dialect that one might encounter in your chosen setting.

NORTHLAND STORIES

LESSON 12: IN A FAR COUNTRY

BEFORE YOU READ

Quote from the Reading

Look for this quote in your reading and pay special attention to its context:

"When a man journeys into a far country, he must be prepared to forget many of the things he has learned, and to acquire such customs as are inherent with existence in the new land..."

VOCABULARY

Look for these words in your reading:

Adaptability – suited by nature, character or design to a particular use
Vicissitudes – a surprising or irregular change
Badinage – playful banter

READING

Read: *In a Far Country* (Pages 134-149)

NOW THAT YOU'VE READ THE ASSIGNED STORY

Reread the quote above. What "things" and "customs" is the author referring to in this quote?

Answers will vary. Students may include some of the following points: The narrator goes on to say that the men must follow primordial laws and work together with their comrades to survive.

STORY SUMMARY

Summarize *In a Far Country* below. Describe the main characters of the story.
Answers will vary. Student may include some of these points in their answer:
A group of adventurers embark on a difficult trip to the Klondike. Carter Weatherbee and Percy Cuthfert were lazy and refused to help out like the rest of the group. Jacques Baptiste, born of a Chippewa woman and a renegade voyageur led the way for the group. Carter and Percy eventually grow too tired to continue with the group and stay in a cabin together. The men eventually become sick with scurvy and the mad clerk kills Percy Cuthfert with an ax.

DISCUSSION

As you read about Carter Weatherbee and Percy Cuthfert, did you think that the story would end badly for them? What were the clues in the story that led you to think that?
(Answers will vary)

WRITING EXERCISE

Many of Jack London's stories share similar themes. Which of his stories has a theme that is most similar to In a Far Country? Write an essay comparing the themes of the two stories. Include at least two quotes from each story to support your stance.

NORTHLAND STORIES

LESSON 13: THE PRIESTLY PREROGATIVE

BEFORE YOU READ

Quote from the Reading

Look for this quote in your reading and pay special attention to its context:

"O what a fool I was to ever let you wag your silly tongue! Thank your God you are not a common man, for I'd – but the priestly prerogative must be exercised, eh? Well, you have exercised it."

VOCABULARY

Look for these words in your reading:

Indolent – disliking effort or activity
Belligerently – eager to or showing eagerness to fight
Scapegoat – a person or thing taking the blame for others

READING

Read: *The Priestly Prerogative* (Pages 150-162)

NOW THAT YOU'VE READ THE ASSIGNED STORY

Reread the quote above. Who said this quote? What do you think he meant by this quote?
Answers will vary. Clyde said this quote to the priest after the priest talked Grace into going back to her husband instead of leaving with Clyde. (Page 160)

_____
_____
_____
_____
_____
_____
_____
_____
_____
_____
_____
_____

STORY SUMMARY

Summarize *The Priestly Prerogative* below.

Answers will vary. Students may include some of the following points:
The Priestly Prerogative is about a married couple, Grace and Edwin, who are prospectors on the Klondike. Edwin does not treat Grace well, and she decides to leave her husband for another man named Clyde. Father Roubeau talks her out of leaving by reminding her of the vow that she made to her husband and how leaving him would bring shame to her family. The priest later regrets sending her back her husband.

DISCUSSION

According to this story, how were women treated differently than men during the Klondike gold rush?

Answers may vary. Students may include some of the following points: Grace worked hard alongside her husband, but he was given all of the credit for her hard work. Married women were not allowed to stake a claim in the Northwest Territory.

WRITING EXERCISE

Father Roubeau goes to great lengths to convince Grace to stay with her husband. Write a persuasive letter to one of the characters in the story to convince them of anything that you want. Include at least three points to support your position. You may include your own creative ideas in your letter.

NORTHLAND STORIES

LESSON 14: THE WIFE OF A KING

BEFORE YOU READ

Quote from the Reading

Look for this quote in your reading and pay special attention to its context:

"But somehow discontent fell upon him; he felt vague yearnings for his own kind, for the life he had been shut out from – a general sort of desire, which men sometimes feel, to break out and taste the prime of living."

VOCABULARY

Look for these words in your reading:

Obsolete – no longer useful
Renegade – an individual who rejects lawful or conventional behavior
Chivalry – an honorable or respectable way of behaving especially towards women

READING

Read: *The Wife of a King* (Pages 163-178)

NOW THAT YOU'VE READ THE ASSIGNED STORY

Reread the quote above. Who is this quote referring to? Rewrite the quote in your own words.
Answers will vary. This quote is about Cal Galbraith. He was bored in Circle City and desired to explore exciting places about which he had heard rumors. (Page 165)

STORY SUMMARY

Summarize *The Wife of a King* below.
Answers will vary. Students may include some of the following points:
The Wife of a King is about an orphan named Madeline who was raised by the good sisters of the Holy Cross. Cal Galbraith met Madeline when he became sick and was cared for by the sisters. They were married and moved to Circle City. Cal was a good husband, but became discontent with his life in Circle City. He left for adventure, promising his wife that we would return by the first mush ice rain. When Madeline heard strange stories of her husband's doings, she sought the counsel of Malemute Kid. She learned to dance gracefully and speak English. She danced at the opera house, while wearing a mask, to disguise her identity from her husband. He was angry with her, but eventually asked her to dance.

DISCUSSION

What do you think about the plan that Malemute Kid came up with for Madeline to imitate an English woman? *(Answers will vary)*

WRITING EXERCISE

Does *The Wife of the King* remind you of another story where the protagonist disguises his/her identity to accomplish a purpose? Compare Madeline to that character in a one-page essay. Describe what steps each character took to conceal his/her identity. Compare the outcomes and lessons learned in each story.

NORTHLAND STORIES

LESSON 15: THE WISDOM OF THE TRAIL

BEFORE YOU READ

Quote from the Reading

Look for this quote in your reading and pay special attention to its context:

"A few words, my comrades, for your own good, that ye may yet perchance live. I shall give you the law; on his own head be the death of him that breaks it."

VOCABULARY

Look for these words in your reading:

Venerating – with regard to reverential respect or with admiring deference
Reluctant – showing doubt or unwillingness
Expedition – journey or trip undertaken for a specific purpose

READING

Read: *The Wisdom of the Trail* (Pages 179-186)

NOW THAT YOU'VE READ THE ASSIGNED STORY

Reread the quote above. Who said this quote? What "law" was he speaking about?
<u>Sitka Charley said this quote to the other Indians that were traveling with him. The "law" of the trail was to honor the trail as the white man did and not deviate from the trail.</u>

STORY SUMMARY

Summarize *The Wisdom of the Trail* below.
Answers will vary. Students may include some of the following points:
Sitka Charley led an expedition to the Yukon that consisted of Kah-Chucte, Gowhee, Joe Eppingwell and his wife. During the trip, Sitka Charley told the other Indians about the "law and wisdom of the trail." He warned them that if they broke trail, he would shoot them with his rifle. Kah-Chucte and Gowhee were very weak and stopped on the trail to make a fire and drink water mixed with flour. Sitka Charley told the men that they must die for breaking the law. They agreed to their punishment and were shot.

DISCUSSION

What do you think about the way Sitka Charley treated the men that he traveled with? Do you think that he could have done things differently? Explain your answer.
(Answers will vary)

WRITING EXERCISE

Imagine that you are getting ready to go on a road trip with your family and a good friend. You want to prepare your friend for what he/she might encounter while traveling with your family. Explain any rules that your family members follow and ways that they tend to do things. Write out your instructions in the form of a letter, dialogue or short story.

NORTHLAND STORIES

LESSON 16: AN ODYSSEY OF THE NORTH

BEFORE YOU READ

Quote from the Reading

Look for this quote in your reading and pay special attention to its context:

"I will talk of the things which were, in my own way; but you will understand. I will begin at the beginning, and tell of myself and the woman, and, after that, of the man."

VOCABULARY

Look for these words in your reading:

Irrelevantly – not relevant or pertinent
Lore – a particular body of knowledge or tradition
Schooner – a ship with a fore-and-aft rig and two more masts

READING

Read: *An Odyssey of the North* (Pages 187-217)

NOW THAT YOU'VE READ THE ASSIGNED STORY

Reread the quote above. Who said this quote? Who are the woman and man that he is speaking about?

Naass was speaking about Unga and Axel Gunderson.

STORY SUMMARY

Summarize *An Odyssey of the North* below. What do you think is the theme of this story?
Answers will vary. Students may include some of the following points:
An Odyssey of the North begins with Malemute Kid, Stanley Prince, Bettles, Meyer and a large group of men relaxing and talking in Malemute Kid's cabin. There was a mysterious stranger there who seemed familiar to Malemute Kid. On the way to Dawson, the stranger asked Malemute Kid for some money and promised to make him rich. Malemute Kid learns that the stranger is an Indian chief named Naass when he comes to Kid's house with stab wounds and acting mad. He proceeds to tell Kid the story of how Axel Gunderson took away his wife, Unga.

DISCUSSION

Why do you think Unga did not want to go back to Akatan with Naass?
(Answers will vary)

WRITING EXERCISE

There are many ways to tell a story. In *The Odyssey of the North*, Jack London allows his character Naass to tell the backstory that explains who he is and what happened to him. Write your own short story employing the use of a backstory. Imitate Jack London by beginning your story with some unanswered questions, and then allow one of your characters to fill in the blanks with a backstory.

NORTHLAND STORIES

LESSON 17: TO BUILD A FIRE

BEFORE YOU READ

Quote from the Reading

Look for this quote in your reading and pay special attention to its context:

"Nevertheless he was aware of a thrill of joy, of exultation. He was doing something, achieving something, mastering the elements. Once he laughed aloud in sheer strength of life, and with his clenched fist defied the frost. He was its master."

VOCABULARY

Look for these words in your reading:

Precept – a command or principle intended especially as a general rule of action
Mishap – an unfortunate accident
Foresight – the act or power of foreseeing

READING

Read: *To Build a Fire* (Pages 218-225)

NOW THAT YOU'VE READ THE ASSIGNED STORY

Reread the quote above. What would you say to Tom Vincent about this quote after reading this story? *(Answers will vary)*

STORY SUMMARY

Summarize *To Build a Fire* below. Why does the story start and end with the precept, "Never travel alone!"?

Answers will vary. Students may include some of the points below:
Tom Vincent set off to travel 30 miles with a wolf-dog to meet his friends who were prospecting despite warnings from the old man that he shouldn't travel alone. It was so cold that the man's face, fingers and toes become frostbitten. He unwisely built a fire under a tree, and the snow from the tree created an avalanche that put out his fire. His fingers became too numb to start another fire. He burned his own flesh to start a fire and attempt to restore circulation. The next day he was able to limp into the camp. At the end of the story, Tom learned that the wise old man was correct; never travel alone.

DISCUSSION

At the beginning of the story, that man is motivated to travel 30 miles to meet his friends. How did his motivation change throughout the story? Why?

Answers may vary. Students may point out that as he became afraid of dying, his motivation became survival, rather than meeting with his friends.

WRITING EXERCISE

Write an alternate ending to the story. Will Tom encounter a stranger in his travels? Does his dog somehow help him? Will he survive in your story?

JACK LONDON'S JOURNEY

LESSON 18: TOWARD FAME AND FORTUNE

READING

Read: *Toward Fame and Fortune* (Pages 226-272)

COMPREHENSION QUESTIONS

1) What was Jack London's birth name? Why was his name changed to Jack London? Where was he born?
Jack London was born in San Francisco as John Griffith Chaney on January 12, 1876. His name was changed to Jack London when his mother, Flora Wellman, married John London. John Griffith Chaney became known as Jack London to differentiate between he and his stepfather. (Pages 226, 238)

2) Was Jack London's prospecting trip in 1897 successful? How did he finance the trip?
He convinced his sister and her husband to grubstake his trip. When they arrived at Dawson City, they learned that all of the good mining claims were taken. Jack and his partners eventually staked a claim on the Stewart River. He developed scurvy from a lack of vitamin C. Realizing that mining was not for him, he gave up the following spring and moved back to California. (Pages 226-235)

3) Name two of Jack London's strongest literary influences?
Answers will vary. Students might include the following: Washington Irving's "Alhambra", Signa, or Librarian Ina Coolbirth, who encouraged his learning. (Pages 238, 250-251)

4) How did Jack London begin his writing career? What were some of the obstacles that he faced to becoming a writer?
Jack's mother encouraged him to submit an article to the San Francisco Call while in school. He won first prize, but was working 13 hours a day and was unable to devote much time to his writing. When he was in the Klondike, he began submitting his writings to several newspapers. He received a lot of rejections. He didn't know anyone who had published his/her works nor did he know much about the publishing process. He eventually received $5 for a story in the Californian magazine. His first book was published in 1900. (Pages 250-255)

DISCUSSION

Which Jack London story is your favorite and why? *(Answers will vary)*

A Thousand Deaths

In the story, *A Thousand Deaths*, who died a thousand deaths? Did the ending surprise you?

Answers will vary. Students may include some of the following points: The protagonist "died a thousand deaths" as an assistant for his father who ran scientific experiments on him. The experiments often resulted in the protagonist needing to be resuscitated.

FINAL ESSAY

Write your final essay on one of the following topics:

1) How did the events in Jack London's life influence his writing? Give specific examples from the stories that you read and the facts that you learned about him in the biography lesson.

2) Write an essay describing three reoccurring themes that Jack London wrote about in his stories. Conclude with your opinion on why he often wrote about these particular themes.

3) As we learned in the biography lesson, Jack London did not have an easy road to become a famous writer. Write an essay about his journey to becoming a writer. How did he start writing? Did he have success right away? Describe his work ethic.

Northland Vocabulary
Crossword Puzzle

Read the Across and Down clues and fill in the blank boxes that match the number on the clues

ACROSS
2   A person or thing taking the blame for others
4   A particular body of knowledge or tradition
6   A person or a thing out of place in time
8   Nearness in place or time
9   An unfortunate accident
11 Showing doubt or unwillingness
13 Disliking effort or activity
14 A surprising or irregular change
16 Relating to a primitive or early age
17 A ship with a fore-and-aft rig and two more masts
19 An act or instance of protest
21 Contradictory or opposed to common sense
22 Something different, abnormal or strange
23 Pity or sympathy
24 With regard to reverential respect or with admiring deference
25 Boring from being always the same
27 An honorable or respectable way of behaving especially towards women
28 An individual who rejects lawful or conventional behavior
29 Not relevant or pertinent
30 Showing kindly feelings or intentions

DOWN
1   A disease or disorder of the body or mind
3   Stubbornly or annoyingly persistent
5   Journey or trip undertaken for a specific purpose
7   No longer useful
10 Playful banter
12 Suited by nature, character or design to a particular use
15 A division of society based upon differences of wealth, rank, or occupation
18 Eager to or showing eagerness to fight
20 The act or power of foreseeing
26 A command or principle intended especially as a general rule of action

Northland Vocabulary
Crossword Puzzle Key

Read the Across and Down clues and fill in the blank boxes that match the number on the clues

Across:
2. SCAPEGOAT
4. LORE
6. ANACHRONISM
8. PROPINQUITY
9. MISHAP
11. RELUCTANT
13. INDOLENT
14. VICISSITUDES
16. PRIMEVAL
17. SCHOONER
19. REMONSTRANCES
21. PARADOXAL
22. ANOMALY
23. RUEFULLY
24. VENERATING
25. MONOTONOUS
27. CHIVALRY
28. RENEGADE
29. IRRELEVANTLY
30. BENIGNANTLY

Down:
1. MADY
3. PETTINACY
5. EXPEDITION
7. OBSOLETE
10. BAITING
12. ATAT
15. CASTE
18. BLIGERENTLY
20. FREESIGHT
26. PRECEPT

How to Grade the Assignments

Our rubric grids are designed to make it easy for you to grade your students' creative writing assignments, story summaries, and discussion questions. Encourage your students to look at the rubric grid before completing an assignment as a reminder of what an exemplary assignment should include.

You can mark grades for each assignment on the last page of the lesson in the student workbook. Use these pages as a tool to help your students track their progress and improve their assignment grades.

Comprehension Questions

Comprehension questions test the students' ability to understand important themes in the assigned reading. Students are given 10 points for every correct answer. You can give 5 points for partial credit. Mark these points on the last page of each lesson in the student workbook.

Discussion Questions

Discussion questions allow students to express their opinion about the reading assignment or related topics. Students are given 10 points for every discussion question that appropriately answers the question. You can give 5 points for partial credit. Mark these points on the last page of each lesson in the student workbook.

Story Summaries

Students are given up to 40 points for each correct story summary. Use the story summary rubric grid on page   as a guide to assign between 10-40 points for each summary. Mark these points for each summary on the last page of each lesson in the student workbook.

Writing Assignment

Students will complete one writing assignment in each lesson. Use the writing assignment rubric grid on page   as a guide to give up to 10 points in each category for every essay. Mark these points for each writing assignment on the last page of each lesson in the student workbook.

Students are graded on a scale of 2-10 in five categories:

1) Originality and creativity
2) Overall organization
3) Word choice and style
4) Neatness
5) Grammar and spelling

Rubric for Writing Assignments

	Beginning 2	Needs Improvement 4	Acceptable 6	Accomplished 8	Exemplary 10
Originality and Creativity	Student made no attempt to write a creative or original piece	Student attempted to focus on the assigned theme, but lacks creativity	Student's work shows some creativity and originality	Student's work is creative, original and on topic	Student took ownership of the assignment to make it his/her own original piece
Overall Organization	Student's work is unorganized	Student's work is somewhat organized	Student's work is generally organized with a few minor issues	Student's work is well organized	Student demonstrated extra care in organizing the assignment
Word Choice and Style	Student's writing is confusing and lacks personal style	Student's work is clear, but lacks personal style	Student's work is clear and shows some personal style	Student's word choice and style is effective and appropriate	Student uses expressive style and sophisticated word choice
Neatness	Student's work is sloppy	Student's work is somewhat neat	Student's essay is mostly neat	Student's work is neat	Student demonstrates extra care making it neat
Grammar and Spelling	Student's work contains several grammar and spelling mistakes which makes it hard to understand	Student's work contains some grammar, spelling and punctuation mistakes, but not enough to impede understanding	Student's work contains only 1 or 2 grammar, spelling or punctuation errors	Student's work contains no grammar, spelling or punctuation errors	Student's work is extremely well-written

Rubric for Story Summaries

Needs Improvement 10	Acceptable 20	Accomplished 30	Exemplary 40
Student's work is incomplete and/or unclear	Student's work includes most of the major points of the story	Student clearly communicates all major points of the story	Student's work is well written and includes all major points of the story

LESSON ONE: INTO THE PRIMITIVE

Comprehension Questions _____ (10 pts. per question – possible 40 pts.)
Discussion Question _____ (possible 10 pts.)

Writing Exercise
    Originality and Creativity   _____ (possible 10 pts.)
    Overall Organization   _____ (possible 10 pts.)
    Language and Style   _____ (possible 10 pts.)
    Composition is neat   _____ (possible 10 pts.)
    Grammar and Spelling   _____ (possible 10 pts.)

          Total _____

LESSON TWO: THE LAW OF CLUB AND FANG

Comprehension Questions _____ (10 pts. per question – possible 40 pts.)
Discussion Question _____ (possible 10 pts.)

Writing Exercise
    Originality and Creativity   _____ (possible 10 pts.)
    Overall Organization   _____ (possible 10 pts.)
    Language and Style   _____ (possible 10 pts.)
    Composition is neat   _____ (possible 10 pts.)
    Grammar and Spelling   _____ (possible 10 pts.)

          Total _____

LESSON THREE: THE DOMINANT PRIMORDIAL BEAST

Comprehension Questions _____ (10 pts. per question – possible 40 pts.)
Discussion Question _____ (possible 10 pts.)

Writing Exercise
    Originality and Creativity   _____ (possible 10 pts.)
    Overall Organization   _____ (possible 10 pts.)
    Language and Style   _____ (possible 10 pts.)
    Composition is neat   _____ (possible 10 pts.)
    Grammar and Spelling   _____ (possible 10 pts.)

          Total _____

LESSON FOUR: WHO HAS WON TO MASTERSHIP

Comprehension Questions _____ (10 pts. per question – possible 40 pts.)
Discussion Question _____ (possible 10 pts.)

Writing Exercise
    Originality and Creativity   _____ (possible 10 pts.)
    Overall Organization   _____ (possible 10 pts.)
    Language and Style   _____ (possible 10 pts.)
    Composition is neat   _____ (possible 10 pts.)
    Grammar and Spelling   _____ (possible 10 pts.)

                                  Total _____

LESSON FIVE: THE TOIL OF TRACE AND TRAIL

Comprehension Questions _____ (10 pts. per question – possible 40 pts.)
Discussion Question _____ (possible 10 pts.)

Writing Exercise
    Originality and Creativity   _____ (possible 10 pts.)
    Overall Organization   _____ (possible 10 pts.)
    Language and Style   _____ (possible 10 pts.)
    Composition is neat   _____ (possible 10 pts.)
    Grammar and Spelling   _____ (possible 10 pts.)

                                  Total _____

LESSON SIX: FOR THE LOVE OF A MAN

Comprehension Questions _____ (10 pts. per question – possible 40 pts.)
Discussion Question _____ (possible 10 pts.)

Writing Exercise
    Originality and Creativity   _____ (possible 10 pts.)
    Overall Organization   _____ (possible 10 pts.)
    Language and Style   _____ (possible 10 pts.)
    Composition is neat   _____ (possible 10 pts.)
    Grammar and Spelling   _____ (possible 10 pts.)

                                  Total _____

LESSON SEVEN: THE SOUNDING OF THE CALL

Comprehension Questions _____ (10 pts. per question – possible 40 pts.)
Discussion Question _____ (possible 10 pts.)

Writing Exercise
    Originality and Creativity   _____ (possible 10 pts.)
    Overall Organization   _____ (possible 10 pts.)
    Language and Style   _____ (possible 10 pts.)
    Composition is neat   _____ (possible 10 pts.)
    Grammar and Spelling   _____ (possible 10 pts.)

                Total _____

LESSON EIGHT: TO THE MAN ON THE TRAIL

Story Summary _____ (possible 40 pts.)
Discussion Question _____ (possible 10 pts.)

Writing Exercise
    Originality and Creativity   _____ (possible 10 pts.)
    Overall Organization   _____ (possible 10 pts.)
    Language and Style   _____ (possible 10 pts.)
    Composition is neat   _____ (possible 10 pts.)
    Grammar and Spelling   _____ (possible 10 pts.)

                Total _____

    Bonus Points for Vocabulary Words Used   _____

LESSON NINE: THE WHITE SILENCE

Story Summary _____ (possible 40 pts.)
Discussion Question _____ (possible 10 pts.)

Writing Exercise
    Originality and Creativity   _____ (possible 10 pts.)
    Overall Organization   _____ (possible 10 pts.)
    Language and Style   _____ (possible 10 pts.)
    Composition is neat   _____ (possible 10 pts.)
    Grammar and Spelling   _____ (possible 10 pts.)

                Total _____

LESSON TEN: THE SON OF THE WOLF

Story Summary _____ (possible 40 pts.)
Discussion Question _____ (possible 10 pts.)

Writing Exercise
    Originality and Creativity   _____ (possible 10 pts.)
    Overall Organization   _____ (possible 10 pts.)
    Language and Style   _____ (possible 10 pts.)
    Composition is neat   _____ (possible 10 pts.)
    Grammar and Spelling   _____ (possible 10 pts.)

                                                                 Total _____

LESSON ELEVEN: THE MEN OF FORTY MILE

Story Summary _____ (possible 40 pts.)
Discussion Question _____ (possible 10 pts.)

Writing Exercise
    Originality and Creativity   _____ (possible 10 pts.)
    Overall Organization   _____ (possible 10 pts.)
    Language and Style   _____ (possible 10 pts.)
    Composition is neat   _____ (possible 10 pts.)
    Grammar and Spelling   _____ (possible 10 pts.)

                                                                 Total _____

LESSON TWELVE: IN A FAR COUNTRY

Story Summary _____ (possible 40 pts.)
Discussion Question _____ (possible 10 pts.)

Writing Exercise
    Originality and Creativity   _____ (possible 10 pts.)
    Overall Organization   _____ (possible 10 pts.)
    Language and Style   _____ (possible 10 pts.)
    Composition is neat   _____ (possible 10 pts.)
    Grammar and Spelling   _____ (possible 10 pts.)

                                                                 Total _____

LESSON THIRTEEN: THE PRIESTLY PERROGATIVE

Story Summary _____ (possible 40 pts.)
Discussion Question _____ (possible 10 pts.)

Writing Exercise
    Originality and Creativity _____ (possible 10 pts.)
    Overall Organization _____ (possible 10 pts.)
    Language and Style _____ (possible 10 pts.)
    Composition is neat _____ (possible 10 pts.)
    Grammar and Spelling _____ (possible 10 pts.)

                                                      Total _____

LESSON FOURTEEN: THE WIFE OF A KING

Story Summary _____ (possible 40 pts.)
Discussion Question _____ (possible 10 pts.)

Writing Exercise
    Originality and Creativity _____ (possible 10 pts.)
    Overall Organization _____ (possible 10 pts.)
    Language and Style _____ (possible 10 pts.)
    Composition is neat _____ (possible 10 pts.)
    Grammar and Spelling _____ (possible 10 pts.)

                                                      Total _____

LESSON FIFTEEN: THE WISDOM OF THE TRAIL

Story Summary _____ (possible 40 pts.)
Discussion Question _____ (possible 10 pts.)

Writing Exercise
    Originality and Creativity _____ (possible 10 pts.)
    Overall Organization _____ (possible 10 pts.)
    Language and Style _____ (possible 10 pts.)
    Composition is neat _____ (possible 10 pts.)
    Grammar and Spelling _____ (possible 10 pts.)

                                                      Total _____

LESSON SIXTEEN: AN ODYSSEY OF THE NORTH

Story Summary _____ (possible 40 pts.)
Discussion Question _____ (possible 10 pts.)

Writing Exercise
    Originality and Creativity   _____ (possible 10 pts.)
    Overall Organization   _____ (possible 10 pts.)
    Language and Style   _____ (possible 10 pts.)
    Composition is neat   _____ (possible 10 pts.)
    Grammar and Spelling   _____ (possible 10 pts.)

        Total _____

LESSON SEVENTEEN: TO BUILD A FIRE

Story Summary _____ (possible 40 pts.)
Discussion Question _____ (possible 10 pts.)

Writing Exercise
    Originality and Creativity   _____ (possible 10 pts.)
    Overall Organization   _____ (possible 10 pts.)
    Language and Style   _____ (possible 10 pts.)
    Composition is neat   _____ (possible 10 pts.)
    Grammar and Spelling   _____ (possible 10 pts.)

        Total _____

LESSON EIGHTEEN: TOWARD FAME AND FORTUNE

Discussion Question _____ (possible 10 pts.)
A Thousand Deaths _____ (possible 40 pts.)

Final Essay
    Originality and Creativity   _____ (possible 10 pts.)
    Overall Organization   _____ (possible 10 pts.)
    Language and Style   _____ (possible 10 pts.)
    Composition is neat   _____ (possible 10 pts.)
    Grammar and Spelling   _____ (possible 10 pts.)

        Total _____

www.ingramcontent.com/pod-product-compliance
Lightning Source LLC
Chambersburg PA
CBHW080742250426
43671CB00038B/2842